I0210090

THE PURSUIT OF MORE

GET WHAT YOU WANT FROM LIFE.

by Melissa Reese

The Pursuit of More

Get what you want from life.

ISBN: 978-1-7327804-9-1

Copyright © 2018

by Melissa Reese

All rights reserved. No part of this book may be reproduced or distributed in any form, except for the inclusion of brief quotations in review, without permission in writing from the author.

Printed in the U.S.

TABLE OF CONTENTS

This Book:...v

Introduction: Know this first. 1

Chapter 1: Pursue knowledge. Learn. Take action.
Create a powerful self. 11

Chapter 2: More. It's good, it's bad, it's ugly,
it's beautiful, it's personal, it's
unanimous, it's known and unknown.......23

Chapter 3: Food for thought, at random.....................35

Chapter 4: Pursue action as a practice and
start healing. 41

Reference/Suggestion List: 55

Books:..55

TED Talks: Listed by presenter...............................56

Videos:..57

About the Author: 59

Permission Slip 63

This Book:

We all seem to be in this pursuit of *more* and many people don't even know what this *more* is for themselves. Many have not identified it, or know if more is what they really want. If they do know, and if more is really wanted, there seems to be confusion or agitation of how to get it or attain it. We seem to be in our own way. This book is a reference guide to clearing a path for yourself. It is about getting out of your own way so you can experience your soul's daydreams as a reality.

This book is an introduction on controlling your emotions and not allowing your emotions to control you. It's about learning to not give another person or situation power of and over how you feel, what you feel, and when you feel it. It is about recognizing that we all have fun and happy emotions and we all have difficult emotions. Difficult emotions can be overwhelming, scary, exhausting, and many other things, but they need to be acknowledged, experienced, and excused in order to live a happier, healthier, more fulfilling life. When you are in control of your emotions you are more in control of your behavior. Only when you deal with and own your emotions as your own, and not someone's or something else's fault, can you experience more of what you *do* want — and less of what you don't want.

Letting go of old, negative emotions can have these benefits: more control, more power, more calm, more joy, more happiness, more love, more feelings and experiences of freedom.

The Pursuit of more includes and is not limited to:

Becoming more self-aware. Being more willing to engage in doing the work that will actually bring more of the best things into your life. Doing more of what you truly want to do and less of what you don't want to do. Being more of who you want to be and less of who you don't want to be, and figuring out exactly what that means. It is giving yourself permission and room to figure out your deepest needs and desires. It is caring more about how you think and feel about *yourself* rather than your perception of how others think and feel about you. The pursuit of more is about living your life in more joy, love, happiness, good-health and well-being rather than fear, worry, anxiety, sadness, and pain. When you are more decisive, confident, thoughtful and more content within, you can then project that out. You will get more of what you want out of life and less of what you don't want. You will get more of what you need within your life.

As you allow yourself to journey in your pursuit of more, allow yourself to be come aware of the people, things and situations that are currently in your life. Allow yourself to notice if you need <u>more</u>: sleep, quality-time alone, exercise, reading time, time out in nature, time to start or finish those "projects" you've been meaning to do and really want to do. (You can not create more time, but you can reallocate it.)

What illusions are holding you back? Do you have false beliefs of not feeling good enough, smart enough, less than, inadequate, unlovable, unworthy, and/or worthless? Are there toxic people that you are keeping around because you have a false belief that you have to? Are there activities that you are allowing yourself to engage in that are the opposite of helpful? Are you allowing yourself to stay at a job that you hate or in a work environment that is less than encouraging? Are you allowing other people's voices to drowned out your own voice? Are you allowing yourself enough time to play, be creative, and engage your 'inner-kid?'

Allow yourself to really take in the information shared on the following pages. *Journal or take notes as you read.* In the last chapter you will have the opportunity to work through some of your 'stuff' by utilizing the exercises I have provided. The exercises may seem simple, and they are very effective when utilized and implemented.

"What's happening is merely what's happening. How you feel about it is another matter."
—Neale Donald Walsch

❖

KNOW THIS FIRST.

We live in a society where emotions, not logic, are in rule. Emotions tend to be reactionary, not necessarily responsive. Logic tends to be more responsive than reactionary. The key is to have these two in alignment, to have them operating in unity at the same time. Our emotions determine much of our behavior, if not most of our behavior. When we are in control of our emotions, we can better control our behavior.

When people talk politics, religion, health and family they typically use emotion more heavily than logic. One, because it's instinctual and these can be emotional topics. Two, emotion is an attempt to navigate the situation or "conversation" of which they logically know nothing about. Three, they are so accustomed to only engaging or heavily engaging emotions because they have no control over them. This typically turns a conversation into an argument, debate, flat-out fight, or attempt to manipulate the person into coming over to their side. Advertising, political campaigns, religions, military, and doctors, to name a few, all use emotional manipulation tactics in an attempt to benefit themselves. Sometimes family and friends do this and we even do this to ourselves.

> *Don't be afraid to question "experts" and "authority." We are all human, doing our best, and as we gain knowledge our reality can be changed and altered.*

It is impossible to get away from our emotional selves and it's actually a detrimental thing to completely do so. However, it is imperative to be able to see and know when there may be an emotional imbalance or an emotional tactic-strategy coming at us so we can engage our logic and unify it with our emotions so we can safely navigate our well-being.

It is important to feel and experience *all* emotions. Anger, frustration, sadness, hurt, guilt, pain, even hate can all be completely healthy when one is in a place of awareness with their emotions. We can experience them and then get through them without any casualties. There are always healthy ways to deal with and navigate *any* emotion.

In order to pursue more in your life it is imperative to have your emotions and logic in alignment and for you to know how to navigate them in a healthy way. Chapter 4 will help you with this. Our emotions and logic can align when we work on our subconscious mind. To learn more about our conscious and subconscious minds refer to books by the following authors: Louise Hay, Arielle Essex, Martha Beck, Bruce Lipton. You can also see a deeper explanation in *The Pursuit of Forgiveness*. Here is a brief explanation that is extremely simplified, a bit overgeneralized, but will hopefully help for now. Think of your emotions as your subconscious mind and your logic as your conscious mind. Our conscious mind is our *goal setter* and our subconscious mind is our *goal getter*. All of our experiences are stored in the subconscious. Our subconscious simply takes the path of least resistance and its job is to keep us safe, so we operate from what we *know*. Sometimes what we *know* is what is holding us back. This is the *mind* you will be working with heavily to get rid of your *crap* (baggage). Sometimes what we *know* is so outdated that it does not work with all the things that our conscious mind can dream up, so they don't end up communicating well together. Once you clear out the old stuff from your subconscious you make room for new and better stuff. Then, you can better align your emotions and logic.

Many people believe that they don't have a choice or even know what options are available for navigating, changing, or healing. They feel stuck, forced, tremendously overwhelmed, lost, and confused — not to mention the not good enough, unlovable, less than, and unworthy that perpetuates the above mentioned. Surely you have experienced any one of these states at some point in your life or may even be experiencing any one of them now in at least one area of your life. We have many areas of life, such as: career, family, romantic relationship, religion/spirituality, health, fitness, et cetera. Sometimes our state of mind or emotions are concentrated in one area, sometimes multiple areas, and sometimes one just seeps into another and there is the appearance of all areas being affected.

Keep in mind that we do not know what we do not know. In other words, there are things that exist that we have no idea exist until we learn that they exist. There are many people in places of power that like to keep it this way. Knowledge can be powerful; it can be refuted, and it can change. Knowledge is only truly impactful when it is experiential and transforms into wisdom. Knowledge is a small subset of wisdom. Within all of us lies wisdom. Within all of us are "knowings." In order to tap into this wisdom and knowing, you must practice self-awareness. This means you must be vulnerable, open, honest, kind, and diligent with yourself. You must practice self-forgiveness. You must have a desire to grow and evolve into more than you are at this moment.

> *You must either be open, inspired, and hungry for almost any and all knowledge or uncomfortable in order to really grow and evolve.*

Growing and evolving can be uncomfortable. Sometimes you have to push up against your comfort zone. You will have to make different decisions than you ever have before. You have to learn how to understand yourself in ways you maybe haven't before, and you have to honor that understanding. You will have to know the difference between discomfort and uncomfortable. Both require you to tune into your heart and mind connection, and both require you to hone your intuition. One is a warning. Discomfort is like an alarm, and being uncomfortable is like wearing jeans that are too tight and hug all the *wrong* places.

Think of discomfort as discourse. Discomfort can be a sign to go the other way, stop what you're doing, do something different, and to fully listen to your heart, mind, and body because you're getting messages telling you something is wrong. Discomfort is not something most can live with for an extended period of time.

Being uncomfortable can bring in hyperawareness to ourselves and the world around us. This is an opportunity to dig into that awareness. We get the opportunity to see our strengths. We get to see our ability to either handle something or not, and then calibrate accordingly. This is where the deepest learning can occur, if we are open to it. People can live with being uncomfortable for extended periods of time; it's a matter of courage that determines what type of *uncomfortable* one is willing to continue to entertain.

Here's where you can start to learn and eventually know what you maybe once didn't know or were not aware of before. Here's where you can start to heal and know it is possible to move into a more wonderful life. Here is where — if you commit to yourself to pursue self-awareness and allow your journey to be one of courage, practice, feedback, curiosity, and openness — all that knowledge can be used and implemented to create a life led by wisdom.

What you learn and the lessons you internalize through self-awareness are what will transform your life into one of fulfillment, contentment, peace, healing and wonderful-possibility.

Courage conquers fear.

You will not pursue anything void of fear, but it is not the absence of fear that will create more wonderfulness in your life, it is the presence and engagement of courage. Courage conquers fear. Courage is what will be your fuel on your journey.

Being uncomfortable and courageous will get you to where you want to be. Being courageous and willing to be patient while being uncomfortable will help you be able to pinpoint what that *more* is that you truly want. Being courageous and willing to pursue that *more* is the most precious and transformative gift you could ever give yourself.

The pursuit of *more* encourages all people to know there is more to *you*. You really are more than you think you are. You really can and are capable of doing more than you think. Pursue the depth of *you,* and your soul, heart, and mind will gain an insight that is impossible for anyone else to gain, and even more impossible for anyone else to control. It is a privilege and an honor to be in control of your emotions. To be able to experience what you are feeling, know how to deal with it, and what to do with it is courageous and powerful.

To be human is to experience an array of emotions, some that cannot be labeled or even explained. To be in control of your emotions, to navigate them, and manage them in a healthy way means you allow yourself to experience this array and then not dwell, ruminate, overanalyze, or focus on any one. You allow them to flow in and then flow out, not to be experienced the exact same way over past situations ever again. It also means you experience happier, more joyful, and more loving emotions more often.

Wouldn't it be nice to have a more consistent flow of those *nice* emotions and feelings? Are you ready to be in pursuit of more well-being? Are you ready to know you are more? Ready to be more?

> *Challenge other people and challenge yourself. Do this with the intention of learning something. Do it with an open mind and open heart. Do it for the sake of entertaining a different way of thinking, seeing, living, being, and doing.*

CHAPTER 1:

❖

PURSUE KNOWLEDGE. LEARN. TAKE ACTION. CREATE A POWERFUL SELF.

W e've all heard: The more you have of _____ the more responsibility and problems you have. There is a push and pull with *more*. Going after *it* and getting *it*. Going after it and then balking. Or consuming the mind with the ideology or daydreams of *more* and doing nothing else but think, pray, and wish (with no action). Sometimes when we get more, we don't know what to do with it. We don't know how to keep it, take care of it, and care for it. Sometimes the thought of having more is overwhelming; sometimes enough to give up.

Having more is worth it when it's fulfilling, enjoyable, peaceful, and inspirational. It also does not take much to manage. When it is all of the aforementioned there is a flow and ease that is easy to connect to, get back to, and even stay in. A gentle rhythm if you will.

You can have more of the *right* things and/or more of the *wrong* things. It's up to you to find and decide if more is a good thing or bad thing for you. But first, you must *know* who *you* are in order to decipher this and navigate it.

> *Go within. Rise above the noise. Break up the pity party.*

You are entitled to a short-lived *pity party*. (Keep the 'invitee' list very short.) Sometimes you just have to feel the *bad* and the *crap-tasticness* of a situation in order to really move through it. As an experiencer, you do this and then you move through it. If you are a victim, you will find you throw yourself *surprise* pity parties and invite all you know. You must shed any role of victim in order to be gracefully powerful within yourself. If you are a victim in any area of your life, denounce that now. Anyone who classifies themselves as a victim automatically relinquishes their power and control to whomever or whatever has *done* something to them. The opposite of a victim is an *experiencer*.

An *experiencer* is someone who has simply experienced something difficult or painful and has taken lessons from it, learned, grown, evolved, and does not allow it to dictate, rule, or run their life. They are through it and they are beyond it. They played an active role in the healing of their own mind and heart. An experiencer no longer says, "This happened *to me*." The past happened, and they are not the victim of it. They are a forger of their own future.

The experiencer takes action.

You must *do* to become, you must *do* to get, and you must *do* to have. Success, change, transformation, happiness, joy, love, satiation, relief, and freedom — all require some sort of action. Without action, you accomplish, gain, or attain nothing. Action happens all the time, but the type of action happening has a big impact on what comes from the action and what it produces. It is true that it can take multiple people and multiple attempts to produce a tangible, beneficial, or even feasible outcome or result; but sometimes it does not take much action for something profound to happen.

Something simple, like chewing your food a few more times can be the difference between choking or not, and it can also help you with better digestion. Simply complimenting someone can get you a conversation that leads to a job, a friendship, another beneficial connection, or a smile and a thank-you that changes the course of your day — and theirs. It can be something big, like working with a transformational therapist or life coach, or moving to a new state or country.

Action can be a decision to do or not to do something. By deciding to not engage your negative thoughts, you are taking action and providing space and possibility for healthier, better, more beneficial thoughts to be engaged with. By doing this often enough, you can change the patterns in your brain, body, and entire life. Doing something or doing something different requires choice and decision. This allows for the possibility of your life improving, your life changing and transforming.

> *Interview yourself. Stay open and curious to who you really are. Not all the things you think are what you really think. If there's a thought or belief you don't like, let yourself not like it and then decide what you want to think and believe instead.*

You have the power to decide for yourself; you have that right and that ability. No one can make you feel anything emotionally that you do not choose to feel. If you experience emotions and feelings, it is because you are allowing yourself to experience them. Just because someone says something mean or does something mean, does not mean you have to feel bad, angry, hurt, or sad. You can decide if you want to feel those things frequently or not.

> *We are not robots, we are meant to feel. We are meant to experience. We are also capable of understanding our emotions within an experience.*

It is healthy and imperative to experience all of our emotions so we can become familiar with them. Only when we are familiar with our emotions and feelings can we learn to navigate them. Remember what you experience is unique and yours. This is all a part of the ever-evolving self-awareness process.

> *Inner strength, vulnerability with self, and permission to truly experience you is key.*

Who might be living in your heart or in your mind rent-free? Who have you given *keys* to? Hint: Anyone who can push your buttons or *make* you go from happy to pissed in zero to sixty has a *key*. Or, if you freeze when making a big decision, or continuously make bad decisions and there are one or two people who pop into your head at those moments, they have *keys*. Your heart and mind are not for rent. You are the keeper of your domain. If your domain is not in order, it's up to you to change that. You get to be responsible for your heart and mind and tend to it like no one else ever could or would. If you want more from life, take all the *keys* back or change the lock!

I previously mentioned holding patterns of *pain*. We hold onto traumas from war, assault, and abuse. By holding on to these things we continue to perpetuate the unhealthy pattern that keeps us down and sometimes out. Why let another person or an experience keep you down? Are you the one victimizing yourself? Why let that trauma and pain keep you in fear and from feeling, being, doing, and having what *you* want from life? Take your keys back. No one, and I mean no one, gets to have a key.

You can undo trauma. You can undo pain. You are that strong, and if you think you are not, there are simple and effective techniques in Chapter 4 that you can use to strengthen your mental, emotional, and physical well-being. Your mind and emotions must be worked, just like any other muscle. You don't go to the gym once and expect to be at zero percent body fat and sporting a *six-pack* that makes men and women blush. You must start somewhere; start simple.

You experience your life and life around you the way you want to, always remember that. Only *you* can change or alter the way you experience your life and life around you. Be in charge of your power and be responsible for your power in your life. Choose and decide to navigate and manage your own emotional well-being. Never give that power and control to anyone else.

Never let anyone else attempt to give their power to you. This is where the *blame game* comes in and this is how people are knocked off *pedestals*. Do you really want to be responsible for another person's feelings and emotions? No one should rely on you for their emotional well-being, except maybe if they are your child or a child in your care and are under the age of eighteen. Even then, a human can learn and know they *have permission* and *the right* to navigate their own emotions and to not allow another person to dictate how they feel.

No one can suck you into a fight. No one can make you do drugs. No one can make you angry, and no one can make you hate. Yes, people can inflict physical pain, harm, or abuse; you still get to decide how you want to experience it emotionally. If you want to be sad, angry, hurt, or otherwise, that is allowed, and even good in order to move through the experience. But if you hold onto it and choose to experience it everyday and more often, then you are allowing that person and that experience to *call the shots, be in charge* and have more power over your emotional well-being than you do.

You can choose to let the anger, hurt, pain, sadness, grief, envy, or jealousy flow in and then move it through and out, letting it go. Definitely do not take it out on anyone, or the cycle of unhealthy behavior and amped-up emotion continues; that is not beneficial. There are ways to let it all go and come through the other side, feeling and doing better. There are exercises listed in Chapter Four of this book. (You can also go to *www.thepursuitofforgiveness.com* to get Forgiveness Process recordings.)

When you have allowed the *unhealthy*, discomfort and even uncomfortable to move through, you have made the choice or decision to be in control of your well-being. You can then think more clearly, behave in a healthier manner, and continue to make better decisions and choices. Just by allowing this to happen one time it allows you to know it's possible, and it makes the next times more bearable and hopeful. You also learn to be okay with the uncomfortable times because you know they are times of growth, transformation, and learning.

Do you see how you can create patterns that are healthy or negative and the choices you make influence this? You can create an unhealthy pattern and give up your power or you can create a healthy pattern and own your power, making it easier to navigate the life you want. You then get to be more creative in how you continue to create and manage a healthier lifestyle and have more fun more often.

We keep ourselves in trauma and in pain when we resist learning and engage coping mechanisms, processes, and techniques. Everyone has experienced trauma. Everyone has experienced pain. Everyone has experienced some sort of mental, emotional, or physical abuse. The difference between those who get through it and those who continue to live it is the ability, as well as the want and desire, to do the work. Someone can believe they are unworthy, unlovable, and less than, and still make the decision to do something different. They are so tired of and done with feeling that way or experiencing it that they must do something different.

Unless there is serious brain damage or a very low IQ, the difference between healing and not healing mentally and emotionally —sometimes physically — is a desire, a want, and a determination. Each person has a knowing or intuition that there has to be something more. There has to be something better than what you are experiencing. What do you want instead?

When going through the healing process, people often still focus on the problem that keeps them in pain and in trauma. You must help yourself for the sake of helping *your whole self*, not just to *fix* the problem you are *momentarily* experiencing. When seeking healing and focusing only on the problem, even though you are doing all the *right* things, you are still fixated on the problem. It can become magnified or more complex instead of eradicated.

For instance, if you are only focused on healing and eradicating the multiple sclerosis, cancer, or EBV effecting you, and not *yourself* —meaning the whole of you and all your emotions — then you are focused only on the problem. You are not focused on the bigger picture. Who are you beyond what you are simply experiencing? What more could your life be? You hold the patterns, which means you hold the *key* to your healing. If you can get yourself into anger, anxiety, fear, worry, doubt, shame, guilt, or pain, you can also get yourself to happiness, joy, love, hope, freedom, well-being, appreciation, and gratitude.

If it seems daunting to do this all by yourself, seek, search, find individuals, groups, or organizations that have a sole purpose to uplift, encourage health and happiness, and encourage *you* to explore and find what brings meaning or at least peace into *your* life, whether it's exactly what they're doing or not. Find what feels good to you, trust your gut (your intuition). When something doesn't seem to mesh or match with you,

stop it and find something that does mesh or match. (Here are some places that I know of: Celebrate Your Life Events, The Empowerment Partnership, yoga classes, meditation groups, Meet Up groups.)

CHAPTER 2:

❖

MORE. IT'S GOOD, IT'S BAD, IT'S UGLY, IT'S BEAUTIFUL, IT'S PERSONAL, IT'S UNANIMOUS, IT'S KNOWN AND UNKNOWN.

More stuff, more material things, more people, more money, more travel, more pets, more food — or really more of most things — is not necessarily a good thing. One can have too much; knowing where that line is, is important. Knowing when more of something is needed is just as important. You find that line and you find that knowing by action. Practice self-awareness, practice self-acceptance, and apply lessons and knowledge.

There is a small list of things you can *always* have more of: love, self-awareness, wisdom, happiness, joy, fun, and gratitude. Outside of these, *more* is to be calibrated by the individual entertaining the idea. *More* is not to be projected by society, culture, religion, tribes, family, or anyone or anything else.

This concept of *more* can be the crumbling of soul, spirit, equality, and dignity if it is not right for you and your well-being. You will know this because as you gain *more,* you will either experience more love, joy, happiness, contentment, and freedom, or not. The concept of *more* can be disempowering when misused or misunderstood. The only way to rise above, or just simply rise to the life you need, want, desire, or hope for, is by empowering your emotional well-being. Calibrate by taking a step back and observing you and your life. Only invite and nurture more self-awareness and more emotional control.

Start by asking yourself questions and give yourself permission to answer *honestly.* After all, you have yourself to answer to. It doesn't matter if anyone else listens to you or really hears you; it does matter that you listen to and hear *you. Be* there for you. If you imagined yourself as a child, how would you be there for that little you? How would you support that little you?

In order to have more of what you want, you have to engage in actions and behaviors that will help in the possibility of the desired outcome.

Here are some ideas:

+ If you don't really feel you know who you are or what you want or need more of, start be reacquainting with *you*. Take time to be with yourself in silence. Think about things that sound like or feel like fun, no matter how *childish*. Ask yourself questions that help you to get to know you. Like, what is your favorite color, food, or game? If you could go anywhere in the world, where would it be? Do you even like to travel? Who in your life do you enjoy to be around the most? Who in your life do you feel energized by, versus depleted by when you are around them (or even think about them)? Get to know *you*!

+ Let more of the *discomfort* and the *pain* go. It does no good to hold on to it. It's okay to be a bit uncomfortable.

+ Find a baby picture of yourself. If you don't have one, imagine a young version of you. Look at and talk to that little you each day. Speak encouragingly, speak with love, speak with dignity, speak with support and care. What does that little you need and want to hear (that they may have never heard)?

+ You are the only one who gets to be in control of your own emotions. Give yourself permission to be the operator for yourself. Remember to never allow anyone else that kind of power and control over you.

+ Other people may not be nice or *play* nice, but that does not mean you need to join them, do the same, or even allow them to infiltrate your emotions or mind. You get to be nice and *play* nice; you are in charge of you.

+ True happiness, joy, and love never come at the expense of someone else's pain, loss, joy, or happiness.

+ Think more about the actions and behaviors that lead to less trouble, less danger, and are less detrimental. Choose to avoid actions and behaviors that lead to potentially *bad* situations.

+ Do more things that are healthy for your body and mind, such as: run, yoga, tai chi, qigong, ride a bike, swim, hike, meditate, eat organic food, eat more fruits and vegetables, drink more water, smile more, dance more, swing, draw, color, paint, volunteer, sing, laugh with joy… These are just some ideas.

+ Focus on more beauty, happiness, and kindness. Continue to do your best to find something pretty, beautiful, kind, fun, joyful, sweet, playful, and loving each and every day. The more you seek this out the more you will find it, see it, and want to engage in and with it.

+ Do your best to be nice kind when another is not nice, kind, or loving.

+ Do your best to separate yourself from people and situations that are detrimental, toxic, dangerous, unhappy, or anything that is not beneficial to your well-being and safety.

+ Do your best to find help. Momentary help is just that, momentary. It can be helpful for acute or immediate need, and then ask to find help that is long-term, life-changing, and will provide stability.

+ Be willing to contribute when receiving help. Provide assistance or help back to the person helping you, or pay it forward and help another. Be involved in your life, in the process of healing and in creating the environment you surround yourself with.

+ Do your best to find people you can talk to about your dreams, wishes, wants, and desires. Especially discuss this *with* yourself.

+ Help others. Even if it's holding a door, smiling, saying please and thank you, letting someone in your lane during traffic, providing food or water for someone in need, a hug, words of encouragement, or anything you think is kind.

+ Gratitude. Gratitude. Gratitude. Find appreciation everywhere.

When you do get *more*, take a moment to step back and observe. Is this "the more" that you wanted or not? If you did get more of what you wanted, are you sure it is still what you want? Does something need to be changed, tweaked, or redone? By taking a step back from time to time to observe ourselves and our lives, we can calibrate better on where we are and then think more clearly on where we want to be. If you want or need things to change or be different, then the first place to start is with yourself. Recalibrating *you* is the only way to truly change your life and transform it into what you want it to look like, feel like, and be like. When you recognize that you have gained and incorporated *more* of what you want into your life, give gratitude, be grateful. This will help lock it in.

> *Pause. Recognize. Evaluate. Engage courage. Take Charge.*

We seem to allow ourselves to be so fragile and affected by other people's spoken thoughts. We twist and turn our lives, our own beliefs, our own feelings, and our own way of living to conform to what one person or group of people think. We mostly do this so that we can feel accepted, so that we can feel a part of something, so that we can feel love. Acceptance and love *must* start with you accepting and loving yourself for who you are. Internal validation is key. More often than not, I would say even 99 percent of the time, you will find at least one other person that you don't have to conform to or with. When you allow yourself to be you, you tend to find and/or attract others that are similar. You find your *tribe*.

> *When you love yourself and accept yourself, you find a healthy tribe. You experience even more love and acceptance. Conformity does not exist within a loving tribe.*

I think many feel it's scary to just be themselves because of what other people think. We keep ourselves in misery, grief, shame, and in pain by doing this. The greatest gift you can give yourself is authenticity and *congruency; your feelings match your words. You grant yourself permission to be who you truly are no matter who you are around and no matter what the circumstance. Sometimes the trick can be finding out *who* that person is. If you've put yourself away for so long that you seem to have forgotten who you really are, take a step back and give yourself permission to be reacquainted with *you*.

The more you allow yourself to really be who you are, the more control you will have over your emotions. It's like you stop lying to yourself and are only truthful. When you are truthful, you don't have to remember backtracking to make sure that you're sticking with your *story*. You are not trying to find the *right* emotions or feelings, you are just experiencing them and expressing them. Being the true you allows emotions to flow in and flow out. A wave never stays on the beach it comes upon. Some waves are bigger than others, and sometimes there are more waves, but they still flow back into the sea. If you're noticing that the *flow* is a little on the heavy side for the *negative* emotions, there might be some more baggage to get rid of or deal with. And then sometimes big situations call for big emotion.

Calibrate for yourself by your responses versus your reactions to various thoughts, situations, and interactions. Notice if they feel *healthy* or if they feel overwhelming and out of control. A reaction is purely emotional; it mostly lacks reason and rational mind. A response is using the emotional and rational mind together; you use feeling and intellect to formulate a reasonable answer.

A scenario: A bowl falls to the ground and breaks. If this bowl is just a bowl and you scream expletives, cry, get overly angry and frustrated, allow it to ruin the rest of your day, or even take it out on someone else around you, you probably have some work to do on emotional baggage. If the bowl falls to the ground and brakes and you feel a little frustrated for a moment, you clean it up, and go about the rest of your day without thinking about it, your emotions are probably *in check*. Now, let's say that bowl was your grandmother's. If you feel angry, then sad, and it's on your mind for the remainder of the day, that could be normal if there was sentimental value and it is something not replaceable. Now, if you take this out on anyone around you, or allow this emotion to continue for days on end or longer, you probably have some work to do around your emotional baggage because this is not *flow*.

That scenario uses a bowl, and do you understand that it's not really about a bowl? The bowl is a metaphor. What or whom is that bowl to you?

When it really comes down to it, we all know how we feel. As a child we knew how we felt. We tend to allow others to quiet or abolish that knowing, and then the trust in that knowing fades or gets buried.

The best gift we can give a fellow being is to remind them that they have permission and the right to navigate and dictate their own feelings and emotions.

The best gift you can give yourself is to remind your inner child, and *you* now, that you have permission and the right to know and navigate your feelings and emotions.

Be you. Be authentic. Be *congruent. Be true.

* What I mean by "Congruency/congruent" is to be in alignment with expressing yourself. Your feelings match your words, they are meaningful, 'right' by you, steadfast, unwavering, and within the light you are connected to. (Say what you mean, mean what you say.) When we are congruent with our life, our self, our words, it makes communication and conflict much easier to navigate.

CHAPTER 3:

─────────── ❖ ───────────

FOOD FOR THOUGHT, AT RANDOM.

Here are some random thoughts and ideas that may help you in your pursuit of more. These are meant to encourage you to think, to get to know yourself a bit better, and to engage the possibilities of various perspectives. To become wiser and more powerful within yourself, your perspective must shift. Only different perspectives allow for any kind of change, growth, or transformation.

─────────────────────────────

Where are you operating from today? Fear or love? Fear or respect? Fear or compassion? Fear or kindness? Only you can choose what you let in, and only you can choose what you let out. It is absolutely a choice. If you allow someone or something else to dictate where you operate from, they have way too much power. Operating from fear is the denial or absence of courage. Fear is the absence of true internal power. Fear is divisive, phobic, unkind, judgmental, weak, and debilitating.

———————————————————————

Other people's expectations of you are not your responsibility. You can only feel failure if you too had the same expectations. And if you learned, took something away from "the experience," "got something" from "it," then it's not failure; it's feedback. If you repeatedly do the same thing over and over and never learn anything or realize anything different then it might be failure, but if there has been any recalibration or different way of thinking or doing, then it is absolutely feedback.

———————————————————————

Remember, you really don't know what another person is thinking or feeling. So, to pretend you do and then experience deep emotion over something that has never been verified is futile.

———————————————————————

We are more likely to see, hear, or experience something falsely or misinterpret it rather than experience it in its purest form for what it is and how it happened. Very few things are true and/or absolute. Therefore it is impossible to experience them as such.

———————————————————————

Measurement is inherently flawed. We create what we use to measure by and we can only measure with what we've created. (Just because we can't measure it, does not mean it does not exist.) Be careful of what you measure, how you measure, and who you measure. It's good to have your own "measuring stick" for your life, and don't beat yourself with it.

———————————————————————

Someone else's judgment or opinion of you is really their burden to bear, not yours; unless you believe their opinion and share in the *truth* of it. Then it is for both to bear. You are the one who gets to decide how you feel about yourself and know who you really are, regardless of what anyone else thinks or feels. You get to be the one to make others right or wrong. Only you decide if that opinion or thought is true or untrue. In this, you either know there is no burden for you and you release the burden, or decide to hold the burden.

———————————————————————

You are the culmination of all your healing. You are the light and forgiveness within. You, being the light in your life, helps to light all the paths and illuminate all the directions of possibilities. *Stay associated with yourself and you will never be lost.*

Time is a construct that can lead you astray. We seem to allow ourselves to be bound by it and to it — slaves, prisoners, captives, and compliant. Time can keep us in denial and restrict us from moving forward. It is an illusion we use as an excuse to avoid or simply not engage in the pursuit of more. We continually create denial loops with time. Denying what is, denying what was, denying what could be. We often deny our soul, our purpose, our wants, our needs, our desires, our thoughts, our feelings, our emotions, and our reality based on these things this human-made construct.

Who are you allowing to keep you angry? Who are you allowing to keep you sad? Who are you allowing to keep you feeling helpless? Who are you allowing to keep you in pain? Who are you allowing to keep you uncomfortable? Who are you allowing to keep you fearful or afraid?

_____

It's not about how people see you or even how you want to be seen. People will see you how they want to and can. It's about what *you* want to show. People will interpret that as they may, but most importantly you are showing up how you want to present yourself and showing up for yourself.

CHAPTER 4:

❖

Pursue action as a practice and start healing.

How much of your energy goes to anger, fear, hate, pain, et cetera? What is it accomplishing?

Take your precious, powerful energy and use it to create and immerse yourself into the opposite of what you hate or what angers you or what pains you. If your energy is wrapped up in or consumed by hate and other negative feelings, what's left for the opposite of that? What's left for the good stuff? Redirect that precious, powerful energy and actually see the opposite come to life. Allow your life to thrive and be bigger and better than ever.

Pain is a black hole; the opposite is infinite light. Where do you want to direct your precious, powerful energy? What could you create with it? How could you experience life differently?

When you let go of the hate and painful energy, you will find you move in the opposite direction of it. You move in the direction of possibility and allow for the space to heal, to be happy, to experience more love and more beauty. You also find that you give way less "F's" about things, and begin to really see what matters and what is silly or of no matter. Have you ever stopped to contemplate this? How good could that be?

Darkness can not exist within light. So, as you practice the following exercises, bring in and imagine as much light around you and within you as you possibly can.

Below are some simple exercises to do that will facilitate change, transformation, and healing. You must incorporate these as a daily practice. *Here is where you make a pledge to yourself, your well-being, and the life you want to create. These may seem very simple, but they are not necessarily easy. These tools can have a profound effect if you allow yourself to do the work. Be vulnerable with yourself, be honest with yourself, take the time for yourself, be courageous for the sake of yourself.* (But you know this from what you've just read previously in this book.)

> *Give yourself permission to shift, change, grow, and transform. It starts with want, then being willing, then doing.*

Breathing Technique: Do this for two minutes (minimum) three times a day. You can do this sitting or lying down. (By the way, t*his is a form of easy meditation!*) You can find the video for this technique on my YouTube channel: *The Pursuit Guru.*

Start by crossing at your ankles. (It does not matter which ankle goes over which.) Then, place both arms straight out in front of you with your palms facing one another. Cross your arms over one another at the wrists. Then, turn your hands so that your palms once again face each other and you can clasp your fingers together, like holding your own hand. Now, either place your hands just like this in your lap or see if you can fold your arms at your elbows and bring your hands up into your heart space. If folding your hands up is a bit too uncomfortable, that's okay, just keep your hands crossed and folded in your lap.

The next most important part is the breathing. Breathe in through your nose, and as you do this allow your tongue to rest at the roof of your mouth. When you breathe out, your tongue drops back to the bottom of your mouth and you exhale through your mouth. So, you breathe in through the nose with your tongue at the roof of your mouth and then allow your tongue to drop as you exhale through your mouth. Make sure your breaths are calm and rhythmic. What is meant by rhythmic is a nice slow deep breath in and a nice slow deep breath out, avoid a quick or shallow breath in and deep breath out or quick breath in and quick breath out.

Hot-Air Balloon Process: Do this along with the Breathing Technique. Give yourself at least thirty minutes to really go through the process; you may need more time depending on the work you are doing.

Imagine that there is a hot-air balloon tethered to the ground next to you. Allow yourself to let go of and *dump*, whatever needs to be dumped or thrown into the basket of the balloon. Really allow yourself to *empty* out. Give yourself permission to let go of the past. Give yourself permission to heal from things you've been holding on to for way too long and any perpetual negative emotions. For instance, if you are feeling a lot of anger, feel all the areas in your body that are experiencing anger and allow the anger to empty out into the basket. It may look like words, colors, shadows, or shapes. However it is represented, just allow it to leave you and go into the basket. You can do the same thing with grief, sorrow, fear, hurt, guilt, or other negative feelings.

As you breathe, really allow yourself this time of self-reflection and an awareness of your discomfort, pain, and other roadblocks. Check in with what is holding you back from feeling how you want to feel, or what you want to feel, what you want to do, and how you want to be, even what you want to have. Out with the unhealthy, let it all go into the basket of the balloon. Let it all flow out until you feel like it's all gone.

When you feel like it's all gone, check and ask yourself when you first feel done, "Is all the _____ gone or is there more to release?" If there is more of whatever you've been working through left, keep going until you really feel it's gone. Once you have emptied out, cut the tethers holding the balloon down. Imagine the balloon, with its basket, floating all the way out of the atmosphere. Send it up and away with love; up, up, until it's gone. Imagine once it leaves our atmosphere that it disintegrates and burns up into nothing.

Continue the breathing and bring your breath — and light, if you want, into the areas of the body you feel need a little more attention or healing. Make sure that you focus on breathing in love, gratitude, joy, happiness, forgiveness, or anything else beneficial for your healing; bring it all into the areas of which you just *emptied* out. Check in with yourself to see if the process is complete; you will know, just ask yourself.

Once you feel the process is complete, you can open your eyes and allow yourself to stretch, move around, and just be. Give yourself some time before jumping into the car, a project, errands or chores.

Forgiveness Mantra:

You can do this daily. It is a good and gentle reminder for presence. To be in the present moment is *the* place to be. Presence helps with mindfulness and mindfulness helps with presence. Sometimes it's a good reminder to just take things one step at a time, one day at a time. (To read more about forgiveness you can refer to my book, *The Pursuit of Forgiveness* and my website *www.thepursuitofforgiveness.com*.)

"Just for today, may I treat myself with kindness, in thought and word, and pardon myself when I realize I may have slipped. Just for today, may I show kindness to another, even if it is not reciprocated. Just for today, may I let go of anger and resentment for myself and others. Just for today, may I let go of sadness and hurt and instead seek happiness and joy.

Just for today, may I acknowledge a triumph or success within myself as well as another. Just for today, may I recognize a lesson that another helped me understand and learn. Just for today, may I recognize a lesson that I allowed myself to understand and learn."

Practice Presence:

Use the above outlined Breathing Technique. While breathing focus on one body part: nose, fingernail, toe, earlobe, kneecap, wrist, eyelid, or some other single body part or organ. *Pick one thing*. Notice how it's feeling, notice what you experience when focusing in on that area, no need to think about it, just notice it. You are just bringing attention to it. Stay open and curious to all that you are simply experiencing in that area. You can expand this as you continue the practice and think about bigger areas. You can think about your entire neck, then your neck as it's connected to your head and torso, and eventually you will notice and experience your whole body all at once.

This little exercise is so very effective. When you can hold your focus and attention to one specific area and become aware of what you're experiencing without any other thoughts entering, you will be well on your way to mastering presence. This carries out in all areas of your life. It will allow you to hear more in conversations, lectures, meetings, and when alone. It will allow you to experience life in ways you may have never thought possible.

Presence is awareness and awareness is presence.

A Bit About Meditation:

Meditation is simply a vehicle that helps you get out of sympathetic mode and into parasympathetic mode. What this means is that you go from fight, flee, or freeze, which is the sympathetic operating system, to rest and digest, which is the parasympathetic operating system. Much of the world tends to live in sympathetic mode. Consistently stressed, ruminating over the past, or way over analyzing the future. There's not a whole lot of being in the present moment. Our body was built to be in sympathetic mode when we needed to fight, flea, or freeze in order to save our own life.

When we are in this mode for an extended time, our prefrontal cortex shuts down, our immune system shuts down, and our digestive system shuts down. Our body is utilizing our blood, and the intense chemicals being released to guide us to getting out of wherever it is it wants to remove us from. When we stay in the state long enough, it starts to drastically break our body down. This is why they call stress the silent killer.

The more often you are able to get yourself into the parasympathetic mode — rest and digest — you open your mind, you give your digestive system flow, and you have the ability to boost your immune system. By being in the parasympathetic state, you can practice presence, you can practice mindfulness. The study/ practice of mindfulness simply means the ability to be present without the bombardment of thoughts, and emotions. This is not to say that you will have zero thoughts and this is not to say that you will have zero emotion. It simply means that you are in the present, experiencing and allowing thoughts and emotions to be fleeting.

Mindfulness is the ability to overcome and more easily navigate through tension, stress, and negativity, thus allowing your body and mind relaxation. Mindfulness is being able to associate with yourself, who you are, how you feel, what you need, and how you are connected to this Earth and other living things. Mindfulness is the awareness that there is not only you. Mindfulness is the awareness that you are a co-creator in your life and that you absolutely have the ability to create change within yourself. Mindfulness is the awareness that you are in control of how you feel, how you think, and what you believe.

By practicing meditation you allow yourself to associate with this awareness. Meditation is absolutely a practice and not something that anybody is truly good at right away. It can take a lot of time to learn how to be still, how to connect with your breathing.

It takes determination, a little courage, and willingness to practice meditation in order to associate with your mindfulness. Sometimes when we are silent with ourselves, is when the uncomfortable stuff can come up or we become aware of just how uncomfortable we have been. Our "monkey mind" starts chattering at us, or the aches and pains in our body start yelling at us. This can be off-putting to some and enough to drive them away from wanting to continue the practice. The key is to have tools and techniques that help you to feel and know that you are in control of your mind and your body. You are in control of the "monkey mind," the aches, and the pains.

Some meditations use storytelling, some use only one word, some use chanting, some use movement, and some use laughter. Some meditations are guided, and other times meditation is *reached* when hiking or exercising. There is no one right way to meditate. I encourage you to experiment and practice to find what works for you.

- - - - - -

These simple, yet effective tools can have a profound impact on your life. *Utilize them.* Take action for your pursuit of more. This book offers much of what you need to get started, even if it's just starting to think a bit differently. *Refer to this book as often as you want or need.* Transformation can look and feel big, and transformation can be small. Rejoice in any and all wonderful transformation in your life.

On the next page you will find references containing suggestions for books and videos that continue to help me in my pursuit. Outside of working with a wise professional, this list of books and videos are all anyone could ever need for completely healing and transforming their life.

If you are ready to pursue more healing, well-being, love, joy, happiness, and gratitude, start with the techniques mentioned in this book. When you are ready to make some significant and fast transformations, find a practitioner who specializes in NLP (Neuro-Linguistic Programming), hypnotherapy, and some sort of energy work. Make sure they are well-rounded (meaning they are certified in multiple healing modalities), educated, and a good fit for your personality and your goals.

REFERENCE/SUGGESTION LIST:

Books:

Biology of Belief by Bruce Lipton, PhD

The Honeymoon Effect by Bruce Lipton, PhD

Molecules of Emotion by Candace Pert

The True Power of Water by Masaru Emoto

You Can Heal Your Life by Louise Hay

The Power of TED by David Emerald

Practical Miracles by Arielle Essex

Love, Medicine, & Miracle by Bernie Siegel, MD

Screw It, Let's Do It by Sir Richard Branson

The Virgin Way by Sir Richard Branson

The Pursuit of Forgiveness by Melissa Reese

Presence by Amy Cuddy

The Four Agreements by Don Miguel Ruiz

The Red Book by Sera Beak

The Anatomy of Calling by Lissa Rankin, MD

Mind Over Medicine by Lissa Rankin, MD

Spirit Junkie by Gabrielle Bernstein

The Universe Has Your Back by Gabrielle Bernstein

Finding Your Way In a Wild New World by Martha Beck

Finding Your Own North Star by Martha Beck

The Untethered Soul by Michael A. Singer

Source Field Investigations by David Wilcock

You are a Badass by Jen Sincero

TED Talks: Listed by presenter

Margaret Heffernan

Amy Cuddy

Kelly McGonigal

Dr. Alan Watkins

Susan Cain

Andrew Solomon

Pico Iyer

Lissa Rankin

Apollo Robbins

Brene Brown

Donald Hoffman

Dan Gilbert

Rory Sutherland

Ken Robinson

Simon Sinek

Videos:

What the Bleep Do We Know?

The Cure Is

Choice Point Theory

The Living Matrix

About the Author:

Melissa Reese is a Holistic Practitioner, teacher, author, and speaker. She has a BA in Psychology from Arizona State University and post education from Southwest Institute of Healing Arts, The Empowerment Partnership, and other training programs. She is a Board Certified Clinical Hypnotherapist, Master Practitioner of Neuro-Linguistic Programming, Psych-K Practitioner, Life Coach, and Jikiden Reiki Specialist. She has over 1,800 hours of training, which is more than the majority of people in her field. Her first book is titled The Pursuit of Forgiveness.

She started her journey in the healing arts as an observer, watching her mom and dad transform their lives in a matter of ten days. Then, she became a client. Melissa started mainly with hypnotherapy, and then NLP, Reiki, acupuncture, and herbs. The work she did profoundly helped her transform her life in a very short period of time. She learned how to clear her anger, communicate more efficiently and effectively, and she learned how self-care and self-work are imperative to implement as a regular part of life.

Melissa also learned how be less judgmental and more open and curious to what life and people have to offer. She has learned that forgiveness is at the crux of any and all healing that can take place. She was so impressed with the improvement and transformation accomplished in such a short time that she decided to pursue this field as a career.

Utilizing the tools and techniques that NLP, hypnotherapy, life coaching, Jikiden Reiki, naturopathic medicine, and other modalities offer, she has been able to heal herself of autoimmune issues and other chronic illness. She has learned how to have and invite in healthier relationships and establish very important boundaries that support her life and well-being.

Her mission has always been to learn and grow as a person and a practitioner — creating positive, permanent change in her life. Her passion is to then utilize that experience, knowledge, and wisdom in a practice that encourages and helps to empower others to stand in their power gracefully, creating the best version of themselves.

Melissa helps people break through and clear their sh*t (mental and emotional baggage) so that they can pursue what has seemed out of reach and experience freedom, joy, happiness, and love more deeply and more often.She believes we each have the tools to heal ourselves, and we must first get out of our own way to be able to access and fully utilize them.

She encourages and helps people to CREATE the life they desire to achieve by assisting them in transforming their perceived blocks and barriers and turn them into stepping stones. Within the pursuit lies the journey, and within the journey lies the answers.

Melissa loves the path that she is on, and her goal is to help people who want to positively change their life, whether it be big or small.

PERMISSION SLIP

You have the key, the only key. Use this key to free the worry, the anxiety, the stress, the anger, the sadness, the pain, the hurt, and whatever feels unbearable. Let it walk right on out of you. You are not the cage in which it gets to reside or dwell.

You are freedom and space. You are light.

You never need to ask permission to feel happy, joyful, peaceful, excited, lovable, healthy, confident, or worth it ever again.

This is your forever permission slip to enjoy life, experience love, and navigate life with a mind of freedom. Let go of all that is not somehow related to joy. Bring in all that is joy and do it with a heart filled with love and gratitude.

With Gratitude:

A special thanks to Elizabeth Gilbert for inspiring this part of the book. The exercise of writing letters, including giving permission to and from what will set us free in life, was powerful, profound, unique, and inspiring.

www.ingramcontent.com/pod-product-compliance
Lightning Source LLC
Chambersburg PA
CBHW071123030426
42336CB00013BA/2175

*9 7 8 1 7 3 2 7 8 0 4 9 1 *